Breaking the Big Words

A Syllable Division Activity Series

Volume 3
Syllable Pattern: VC/V
Syllable Types: Cl, Op, ME, VP, BR

Josh Morgan, M.A. Ed.

Literacy Specialist
Special Educator
Intervention Coach

Breaking the Big Words
Volume 3: VC/V

Table of Contents

What is Breaking the Big Words?

Introduction & Overview

The "Breaking the Big Words" Syllabication Activity Series provides scaffolded, research-based instruction on dividing syllables, identifying syllable types, and generalizing the skills to decode words and sentences.

This is the third Volume of the series and focuses on VC/V syllable pattern. There are five activity sets with each successive set introducing a new syllable type. With each set a new syllable type is added to build up to three-syllable words containing any of the six syllable types. Volume four introduces the V/V syllable pattern.

Each set includes strategies for navigating consonant blends and digraphs when dividing syllables with visual supports to prompt students on Versions A and B. These prompts are faded on Version C to ensure students do not become dependent on the prompts. Anchor words are used as a visual support on Versions A and B of the activity sheets to remind students of strategies and the placement of each label. These visuals are faded on Version C. The same anchor words used on the activity sheets are provided as posters for classroom display to reference while reading, spelling, or writing unfamiliar words that may adhere to the syllable pattern.

To ensure skill generalization to basic reading, on the same activity sheet, students break words (slash between syllables) BEFORE reading a word list then WHILE reading sentences. Sight words are controlled in the series and consist primarily of PrePrimer and Primer Dolch words.

Each Activity Set of "Breaking the Big Words" employs three levels of scaffolding, embedded differentiation, a strong visual component, developmentally appropriate activities, and an instructional framework (Scope and Sequence).

Find me on the web!

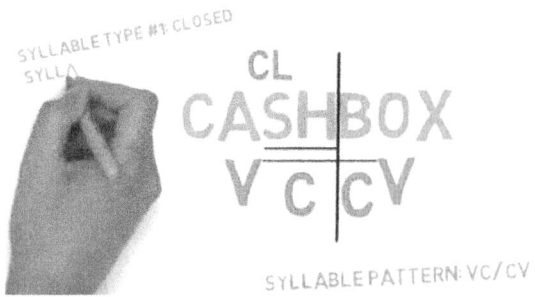

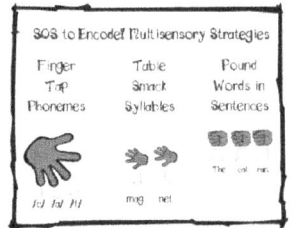

Features of
Breaking the Big Words

Research Based Strategies

- Syllabication: Consistent, systematic procedure for dividing multisyllabic words.
- Syllable Types: Students use a mnemonic device to recall, label, determine vowel sound, and decode syllable types.
- Long and Short Vowels: Labeling and decoding of syllables with long and short vowels.
- Decoding:
  o The last step of syllabication is always to decode the word.
  o Students decode in multiple contexts following syllabication for generalization.

Scaffolding:

- Multiple visual supports are employed to differentiate the activities. This ensures each student is able to work at their level and fosters independence, confidence, and success with the strategy.
- As students gain skills, supports are gradually removed to promote independence.

Components of each activity:

- New Words: Introduced during this activity.
- Review: Familiar syllable types and patterns for practice and maintenance.
- Break before You Read (word list): This step, following syllabication, uses the informal, "break" strategy. Students insert a slash to separate syllables. This occurs prior to reading the words.
- Break While You Read: This activity continues the generalization as students use the "break" strategy. Students read two sentences and "break" words as they come to them.

Beyond BTBW

Add additional levels of generalization

- As students progress through the activity sets incorporate supplemental activities that require students to divide syllables with known syllable types and patterns.

- For example, once students are able to divide words with closed syllables and VC/CV pattern, you can use these words with:
  - Spelling Words by asking the students to...
    - Write spelling words and "Break Before You Read."
    - Write sentences or stories with the words then divide them.
    - Read spelling sentences or stories written by peers and "Break While You Read."

  - Vocabulary Words by asking students to...
    - Break math, science, and social studies vocabulary words before beginning a new unit or chapter.
    - Read a historical text or article and "Break While You Read."
    - Break difficult words in math word problems to help students decode and understand the task.

  - Decodable Passages, Books and Stories by asking to:
    - Find difficult words and "Break Before You Read."
    - "Break While You Read" then reflect with a small group.

  - Tests, Worksheets, & Directions by asking students to...
    - Break words in directions to improve understanding,
    - "Break While You Read" on tests and worksheets to generalize skills to assessments.

Scope & Sequence

- This is Volume 3 and the "Green Set" of activities. Each set will focus on a single syllable pattern and will progress to cover each of the six syllable types within that pattern.
- Syllable patterns are introduced in a specific order to ensure students master a single syllable type with blends and digraphs before moving on to the next type.
- As students reach mastery with recognizing and decoding each syllable type, the next will be introduced.

Full Series

Volume	Color	Syllable Pattern	Syllable Types
1	Red	VC/CV	Cl, Op, ME, VP, BR, C-le
2	Blue	V/CV	Cl, Op, ME, VP, BR, C-le
3	Green	VC/V	Cl, Op, ME, VP, BR
4	Orange	V/V	Cl, Op, ME, VP, BR

Volume 3 Sets 14 to 18

Set	Syllable Pattern	Syllable Types
14	V/CV	Closed & Open
15	V/CV	Open & Closed
16	V/CV	Magic E, Op, & Cl
17	V/CV	Vowel Pairs, ME, Op, & Cl
18	V/CV	Bossy R, VP, ME, Op, & Cl

Common Core State Standards

Print Concepts

K
RF.K.1 Demonstrate understanding of the organization and basic features of print.
RF.K.1a Follow words from left to right, top to bottom, and page by page.
RF.K.1b Recognize that spoken words are represented in written language by specific sequences of letters.
RF.K.1c Understand that words are separated by spaces in print.

1
RF.1.1 Demonstrate understanding of the organization and basic features of print.
RF.1.1a Recognize the distinguishing features of a sentence (e.g., first word, capitalization, ending punctuation).

Phonological Awareness

K
RF.K.2 Demonstrate understanding of spoken words, syllables, and sounds (phonemes).
RF.K.2b Count, pronounce, blend, and segment syllables in spoken words.
RF.K.2c Blend and segment onsets and rimes of single-syllable spoken words.

1
RF.1.2 Demonstrate understanding of spoken words, syllables, and sounds (phonemes).
RF.1.2a Distinguish long from short vowel sounds in spoken single-syllable words.
RF.1.2b Orally produce single-syllable words by blending sounds (phonemes), including consonant blends.
RF.1.2c Isolate and pronounce initial, medial vowel, and final sounds (phonemes) in spoken single-syllable words.
RF.1.2d Segment spoken single-syllable words into their complete sequence of individual sounds (phonemes).

Phonics and Word Recognition

K
RF.K.3 Know and apply grade-level phonics and word analysis skills in decoding words.
RF.K.3a Demonstrate basic knowledge of one-to-one letter-sound correspondences by producing the primary sound or many of the most frequent sounds for each consonant.
RF.K.3b Associate the long and short sounds with the common spellings (graphemes) for the five major vowels.
RF.K.3c Read common high-frequency words by sight (e.g., the, of, to, you, she, my, is, are, do, does).

1
RF.1.3 Know and apply grade-level phonics and word analysis skills in decoding words.
RF.1.3a Know the spelling-sound correspondences for common consonant digraphs.
RF.1.3b Decode regularly spelled one-syllable words.
RF.1.3c Know final -e and common vowel team conventions for representing long vowel sounds.
RF.1.3d Use knowledge that every syllable must have a vowel sound to determine the number of syllables in a printed word.
RF.1.3e Decode two-syllable words following basic patterns by breaking the words into syllables.
RF.1.3g Recognize and read grade-appropriate irregularly spelled words.

2
RF.2.3 Know and apply grade-level phonics and word analysis skills in decoding words.
RF.2.3a Distinguish long and short vowels when reading regularly spelled one-syllable words.
RF.2.3b Know spelling-sound correspondences for additional common vowel teams.
RF.2.3c Decode regularly spelled two-syllable words with long vowels.
RF.2.3d Decode words with common prefixes and suffixes.
RF.2.3e Identify words with inconsistent but common spelling-sound correspondences.
RF.2.3f Recognize and read grade-appropriate irregularly spelled words.

3
RF.3.3 Know and apply grade-level phonics and word analysis skills in decoding words.
RF.3.3a Identify and know the meaning of the most common prefixes and derivational suffixes.
RF.3.3b Decode words with common Latin suffixes.
RF.3.3c Decode multi-syllable words.
RF.3.3d Read grade-appropriate irregularly spelled words.

Fluency	
K	RF.K.4 Read emergent-reader texts with purpose and understanding.
1	RF.1.4 Read with sufficient accuracy and fluency to support comprehension.
2	RF.2.4 Read with sufficient accuracy and fluency to support comprehension. RF.2.4a Read grade-level text with purpose and understanding. RF.2.4b Read grade-level text orally with accuracy, appropriate rate, and expression on successive readings. RF.2.4c Use context to confirm or self-correct word recognition and understanding, rereading as necessary.
3	RF.3.4 Read with sufficient accuracy and fluency to support comprehension. RF.3.4a Read grade-level text with purpose and understanding. RF.3.4c Use context to confirm or self-correct word recognition and understanding, rereading as necessary.

Visual Supports & Scaffolding

Each Activity has three levels or versions.
Level A activities provide highest level of visual supports while Level C provides the least.

Supports	Version A	B	C
Steps for Dividing Syllables	YES	YES	YES
Visual Model with Bridge	YES	YES	NO
Consonant blends/digraphs underlined	YES	YES	NO
Models for Breaking Before and While Reading	YES	YES	NO
Boxes to guide syllable division	YES	NO	NO

Suggested Implementation Options

There are many ways to use this resource. Below are two suggestions with additional details.

Option 1:
- Activities can be distributed to a class or group of students based on their ability to complete the work independently.
    - Students who struggle more would get the version with the most supports while others can get a version with less supports.
    - While pre-teaching or reviewing, all students will have the same words and will be able to follow along with the lesson while using sheets with different levels of support.

Option 2:
- Teacher uses all three versions/levels with all students each week to scaffold the entire group together (small or whole group).
    - Students would all have same version of the activity at the same time.
    - During the week, the teacher begins with Version A (most support) and decreases support until students can complete Version C (least support) before moving on.
    - This option is great for small groups and intervention groups with students struggling to read and write multisyllabic words.

Activity Set
14

Syllable Type Focus: Closed

Scope and Sequence

Activity Number	Syllable Pattern	1st Syllable Type	2nd Syllable Type	3rd Syllable Type	Phonics
1	VC/V	Cl	Cl	X	Single Phonemes
2	VC/V	Cl	Cl	X	Blends
3	VC/V	Cl	Cl	X	Digraphs
4	VC/V	Cl	Cl	Cl	Single Phonemes
5	VC/V	Cl	Cl	Cl	Blends & Digraphs

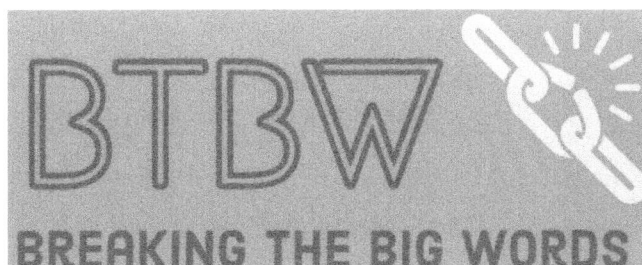

BTBW
BREAKING THE BIG WORDS

11

Follow the steps to divide the syllables.
1. Label the first two vowels.
2. Draw the bridge.
3. Label consonants on the bridge.
4. Choose pattern and break the word.
5. Repeat for any other syllables.
6. Label the syllable.

c l   c l
rob|in
V C V

New
Words

robin

comet

cabin

camel

vomit

wagon

Break BEFORE you read

rob/in
comet
cabin
camel
vomit
wagon

Break WHILE you read

We saw the rob/in and the comet at the cabin.

Did that camel just vomit in the wagon?

Name: _____

Follow the steps to divide the syllables.
1. Label the first two vowels.
2. Draw the bridge.
3. Label consonants on the bridge.
4. Choose pattern and break the word.
5. Repeat for any other syllables.
6. Label the syllable.

c| c|
ro b|in
V C |N

New
Words

robin   comet

cabin   camel

vomit   wagon

Break BEFORE you read   Break WHILE you read

rob/in
comet   We saw the rob/in and
cabin   the comet at the cabin.
camel
vomit   Did that camel just
wagon   vomit in the wagon?

Name: ________________________________ Activity 14.1 Version: C

Follow the steps to divide the syllables.

1. Label the first two vowels.
2. Draw the bridge.
3. Label consonants on the bridge.
4. Choose pattern and break the word.
5. Repeat for any other syllables.
6. Label the syllable.

New Words

robin comet

cabin camel

vomit wagon

Break BEFORE you read

robin
comet
cabin
camel
vomit
wagon

Break WHILE you read

We saw the robin and the comet at the cabin.

Did that camel just vomit in the wagon?

Follow the steps to divide the syllables.
1. Label the first two vowels.
2. Draw the bridge.
3. Label consonants on the bridge.
4. Choose pattern and break the word.
5. Repeat for any other syllables.
6. Label the syllable.

dragon

New Words

dragon

closet

present

planet

Review

metal

lemon

Break BEFORE you read

drag/on
present
closet
planet
metal
lemon

Break WHILE you read

The met/al dragon in the closet was a present from Robin.

Will there be dragons on this planet one day?

Follow the steps to divide the syllables.
1. Label the first two vowels.
2. Draw the bridge.
3. Label consonants on the bridge.
4. Choose pattern and break the word.
5. Repeat for any other syllables.
6. Label the syllable.

dragon

New
Words

dragon   present

closet   planet

Review

metal   lemon

Break BEFORE you read

drag/on
present
closet
planet
metal
lemon

Break WHILE you read

The met/al dragon in the closet was a present from Robin.

Will there be dragons on this planet one day?

<u>Follow the steps to divide the syllables.</u>
1. Label the first two vowels.
2. Draw the bridge.
3. Label consonants on the bridge.
4. Choose pattern and break the word.
5. Repeat for any other syllables.
6. Label the syllable.

New
Words

dragon   present

closet   planet

Review

metal   lemon

Break BEFORE you read   Break WHILE you read

dragon   The metal dragon in
present   the closet was a
closet   present from Robin.
planet
metal   Will there be dragons
lemon   on this planet one
                day?

Follow the steps to divide the syllables.
1. Label the first two vowels.
2. Draw the bridge.
3. Label consonants on the bridge.
4. Choose pattern and break the word.
5. Repeat for any other syllables.
6. Label the syllable.

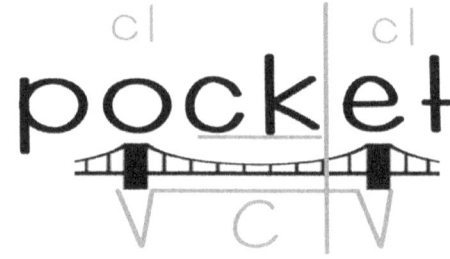

po<u>ck</u>et

☐ ☐

lo<u>ck</u>et

New Words

☐ ☐

<u>cri</u><u>ck</u>et

Review ☐ ☐

seco<u>nd</u>

☐ ☐

po<u>ck</u>et

☐ ☐

bu<u>ck</u>et

☐ ☐

<u>cli</u>nic

Break BEFORE you read

lock/et
pocket
cricket
bucket
second
clinic

Break WHILE you read

I put the sec/ond locket in my pocket.

How did the cricket get stuck in the bucket?

Follow the steps to divide the syllables.
1. Label the first two vowels.
2. Draw the bridge.
3. Label consonants on the bridge.
4. Choose pattern and break the word.
5. Repeat for any other syllables.
6. Label the syllable.

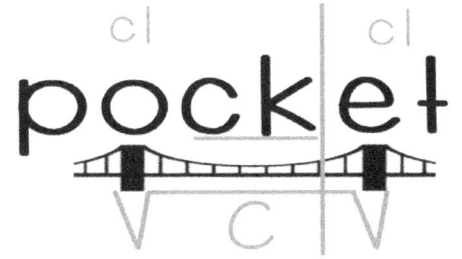

pocket

New Words

locket   pocket

cricket   bucket

Review

second   clinic

Break BEFORE you read

lock/et
pocket
cricket
bucket
second
clinic

Break WHILE you read

I put the sec/ond locket in my pocket.

How did the cricket get stuck in the bucket?

Follow the steps to divide the syllables.
1. Label the first two vowels.
2. Draw the bridge.
3. Label consonants on the bridge.
4. Choose pattern and break the word.
5. Repeat for any other syllables.
6. Label the syllable.

New
Words

locket   pocket

cricket   bucket

Review

second   clinic

Break BEFORE you read   Break WHILE you read

locket

pocket   I put the second locket
                           in my pocket.
cricket

bucket   How did the cricket get
                           stuck in the bucket?
second

clinic

Name: _____

Activity 14.4   Version: A

Follow the steps to divide the syllables.

1. Label the first two vowels.
2. Draw the bridge.
3. Label consonants on the bridge.
4. Choose pattern and break the word.
5. Repeat for any other syllables.
6. Label the syllable.

cl | cl | cl

vol|can|ic

VCCVCV

New Words

□ □ □
volcanic

□ □ □
exotic

□ □ □
inhabit

Review

□ □
ticket

□ □
static

□ □
finish

Break BEFORE you read

vol/can/ic
exotic
inhabit
ticket
static
finish

Break WHILE you read

His class will collect as much of the vol/can/ic rock as they can today.

An exotic dragon inhabits the cabin on top of the hill.

Follow the steps to divide the syllables.
1. Label the first two vowels.
2. Draw the bridge.
3. Label consonants on the bridge.
4. Choose pattern and break the word.
5. Repeat for any other syllables.
6. Label the syllable.

vol|can|ic
VCCVC

New Words

volcanic

exotic

inhabit

Review

ti<u>ck</u>et

<u>st</u>atic

fini<u>sh</u>

Break BEFORE you read

vol/can/ic
exotic
inhabit
ticket
static
finish

Break WHILE you read

His class will collect as much of the vol/can/ic rock as they can today.

An exotic dragon inhabits the cabin on top of the hill.

<u>Follow the steps to divide the syllables.</u>
1. Label the first two vowels.
2. Draw the bridge.
3. Label consonants on the bridge.
4. Choose pattern and break the word.
5. Repeat for any other syllables.
6. Label the syllable.

New Words

	Review
volcanic	ticket
exotic	static
inhabit	finish

Break BEFORE you read

volcanic
exotic
inhabit
ticket
static
finish

Break WHILE you read

His class will collect as much of the volcanic rock as they can today.

An exotic dragon inhabits the cabin on top of the hill.

Follow the steps to divide the syllables.
1. Label the first two vowels.
2. Draw the bridge.
3. Label consonants on the bridge.
4. Choose pattern and break the word.
5. Repeat for any other syllables.
6. Label the syllable.

cl   cl   cl
athletic
V C C V C V

New Words

□ □ □
a t h l e t i c
[ ]

□ □ □
c o l o n i s t
[ ]

□ □ □
e v i d e n t
[ ]

Review

□ □
r a c k e t
[ ]

□ □
t a l e n t
[ ]

□ □
s o l i d
[ ]

Break BEFORE you read

ath/let/ic
colonist
evident
racket
talent
solid

Break WHILE you read

The ath/let/ic colonist took the racket for the match.

Her class work was evident in the on the habitat quiz.

Follow the steps to divide the syllables.
1. Label the first two vowels.
2. Draw the bridge.
3. Label consonants on the bridge.
4. Choose pattern and break the word.
5. Repeat for any other syllables.
6. Label the syllable.

athletic

New Words

athletic

colonist

evident

Review

racket

talent

solid

Break BEFORE you read

ath/let/ic
colonist
evident
racket
talent
solid

Break WHILE you read

The ath/let/ic colonist took the racket for the match.

Her class work was evident in the on the habitat quiz.

Follow the steps to divide the syllables.
1. Label the first two vowels.
2. Draw the bridge.
3. Label consonants on the bridge.
4. Choose pattern and break the word.
5. Repeat for any other syllables.
6. Label the syllable.

New Words

Review

athletic

racket

colonist

talent

evident

solid

Break BEFORE you read

athletic
colonist
evident
racket
talent
solid

Break WHILE you read

The athletic colonist took the racket for the match.

Her class work was evident in the on the habitat quiz.

Activity Set 15

Syllable Type Focus: Open

Scope and Sequence

Activity Number	Syllable Pattern	1st Syllable Type	2nd Syllable Type	3rd Syllable Type	Phonics
1	VC/V	Cl	Op	X	Single Phonemes
2	VC/V	Cl	Op	X	Blends & Digraphs
3	VC/V	Cl	Op	X	Blends & Digraphs
4	VC/V	Cl	Cl	Op	Single Phonemes
5	VC/V	Cl	Cl	Op	Blends & Digraphs

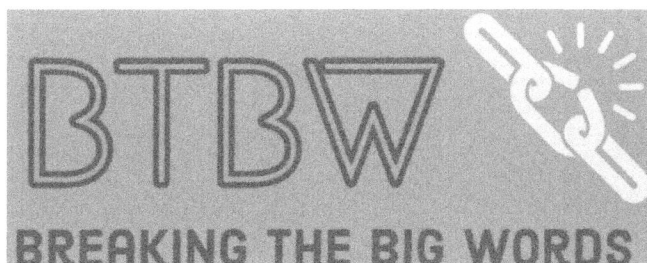

BTBW
BREAKING THE BIG WORDS

<u>Follow the steps to divide the syllables.</u>
1. Label the first two vowels.
2. Draw the bridge.
3. Label consonants on the bridge.
4. Choose pattern and break the word.
5. Repeat for any other syllables.
6. Label the syllable.

New
Words

city

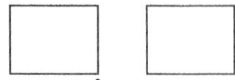

copy

many

lily

body

pity

Break BEFORE you read

cit/y
lily
copy
body
many
pity

Break WHILE you read

The cab/in west of the city has a pond with lily pads.

On the test we got to copy body poses from a sketch.

Follow the steps to divide the syllables.
1. Label the first two vowels.
2. Draw the bridge.
3. Label consonants on the bridge.
4. Choose pattern and break the word.
5. Repeat for any other syllables.
6. Label the syllable.

cl   op
c i t y
VCV

New
Words

city   lily

copy   body

many   pity

Break BEFORE you read   Break WHILE you read

cit/y   The cab/in west of the
lily   city has a pond with lily
copy   pads.
body
many   On the test we got to
pity   copy body poses from a
                               sketch.

<u>Follow the steps to divide the syllables.</u>
1. Label the first two vowels.
2. Draw the bridge.
3. Label consonants on the bridge.
4. Choose pattern and break the word.
5. Repeat for any other syllables.
6. Label the syllable.

city   lily

New
Words

copy   body

many   pity

Break BEFORE you read   Break WHILE you read

city   The cabin west of the
lily   city has a pond with lily
copy   pads.
body
many   On the test we got to
pity   copy body poses from a
                                  sketch.

<u>Follow the steps to divide the syllables.</u>
1. Label the first two vowels.
2. Draw the bridge.
3. Label consonants on the bridge.
4. Choose pattern and break the word.
5. Repeat for any other syllables.
6. Label the syllable.

cl | op
s t u d y
V C V

New
Words

□ □
s<u>t</u>udy

□ □
<u>tr</u>icky

☐

☐

□ □
<u>ch</u>ili

□ □
i<u>tch</u>y

☐

☐

□ □
scra<u>tch</u>y

□ □
s<u>t</u>icky

☐

☐

Break BEFORE you read

stud/y
tricky
chili
itchy
scratchy
sticky

Break WHILE you read

I am glad I sat down to stud/y for the tricky quiz on the body.

The chili made me itchy and my neck scratchy.

Follow the steps to divide the syllables.
1. Label the first two vowels.
2. Draw the bridge.
3. Label consonants on the bridge.
4. Choose pattern and break the word.
5. Repeat for any other syllables.
6. Label the syllable.

cl   op
s t u d y
V C V

New
Words

study

tricky

chili

itchy

scratchy

sticky

Break BEFORE you read

stud/y
tricky
chili
itchy
scratchy
sticky

Break WHILE you read

I am glad I sat down to stud/y for the tricky quiz on the body.

The chili made me itchy and my neck scratchy.

<u>Follow the steps to divide the syllables.</u>
1. Label the first two vowels.
2. Draw the bridge.
3. Label consonants on the bridge.
4. Choose pattern and break the word.
5. Repeat for any other syllables.
6. Label the syllable.

New
Words

study

tricky

chili

itchy

scratchy

sticky

Break BEFORE you read

study
tricky
chili
itchy
scratchy
sticky

Break WHILE you read

I am glad I sat down to study for the tricky quiz on the body.

The chili made me itchy and my neck scratchy.

Follow the steps to divide the syllables.
1. Label the first two vowels.
2. Draw the bridge.
3. Label consonants on the bridge.
4. Choose pattern and break the word.
5. Repeat for any other syllables.
6. Label the syllable.

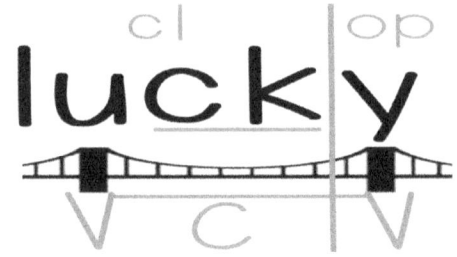

cl   op
lu c k y
V   C   V

New
Words

☐   ☐
lucky
☐

☐   ☐
catchy
☐

☐   ☐
picky
☐

☐   ☐
Ricky
☐

☐   ☐
Chucky
☐

☐   ☐
yucky
☐

Break BEFORE you read

luck/y
Ricky
catchy
Chucky
picky
yucky

Break WHILE you read

We were luck/y the bug Ricky went home with was not catchy.

Chucky is a little picky and felt the snack was yucky.

Follow the steps to divide the syllables.
1. Label the first two vowels.
2. Draw the bridge.
3. Label consonants on the bridge.
4. Choose pattern and break the word.
5. Repeat for any other syllables.
6. Label the syllable.

cl | op
lu c k y
V | V
C

lucky   Ricky

New
Words

catchy   Chucky

picky   yucky

Break BEFORE you read   Break WHILE you read

luck/y   We were luck/y the bug
Ricky   Ricky went home with
catchy   was not catchy.
Chucky
picky   Chucky is a little picky
yucky   and felt the snack was
                              yucky.

Follow the steps to divide the syllables.
1. Label the first two vowels.
2. Draw the bridge.
3. Label consonants on the bridge.
4. Choose pattern and break the word.
5. Repeat for any other syllables.
6. Label the syllable.

New
Words

lucky   Ricky

catchy   Chucky

picky   yucky

Break BEFORE you read   Break WHILE you read

lucky   We were lucky the bug
Ricky   Ricky went home with
catchy   was not catchy.
Chucky
picky   Chucky is a little picky
yucky   and felt the snack was
                               yucky.

Name: _____

Follow the steps to divide the syllables.
1. Label the first two vowels.
2. Draw the bridge.
3. Label consonants on the bridge.
4. Choose pattern and break the word.
5. Repeat for any other syllables.
6. Label the syllable.

cl   cl op
cavity
VCNCV

New Words

cavity

magnify

family

Review

Becky

tacky

patchy

Break BEFORE you read

cav/it/y
magnify
family
Becky
tacky
patchy

Break WHILE you read

Beck/y did not have a cavity at her check up.

In class we got to magnify an ant to see the body.

Follow the steps to divide the syllables.
1. Label the first two vowels.
2. Draw the bridge.
3. Label consonants on the bridge.
4. Choose pattern and break the word.
5. Repeat for any other syllables.
6. Label the syllable.

cl | cl op
cavity
VC|VC|V

New Words

cavity

magnify

family

Review

Be<u>ck</u>y

ta<u>ck</u>y

pa<u>tch</u>y

Break BEFORE you read

cav/it/y
magnify
family
Becky
tacky
patchy

Break WHILE you read

Beck/y did not have a cavity at her check up.

In class we got to magnify an ant to see the body.

Name: _____

Follow the steps to divide the syllables.
1. Label the first two vowels.
2. Draw the bridge.
3. Label consonants on the bridge.
4. Choose pattern and break the word.
5. Repeat for any other syllables.
6. Label the syllable.

New Words

Review

cavity

Becky

magnify

tacky

family

patchy

Break BEFORE you read
cavity
magnify
family
Becky
tacky
patchy

Break WHILE you read
Becky did not have a cavity at her check up.

In class we got to magnify an ant to see the body.

Follow the steps to divide the syllables.
1. Label the first two vowels.
2. Draw the bridge.
3. Label consonants on the bridge.
4. Choose pattern and break the word.
5. Repeat for any other syllables.
6. Label the syllable.

cl | cl | op
gravity
VC|VC|V

New Words

gr**a**v**i**ty

s**y**mp**a**<u>th</u>y

K**e**nt**u**cky

Review

p**a**<u>t</u>ch**y**

<u>sk</u>**e**<u>t</u>ch**y**

p**i**<u>t</u>ch**y**

Break BEFORE you read

grav/it/y
sympathy
Kentucky
patchy
sketchy
pitchy

Break WHILE you read

We felt un/luck/y when gravity made the rocket fall from the sky.

We all felt sympathy for our squad who lost in Kentucky.

Name: _____

Follow the steps to divide the syllables.
1. Label the first two vowels.
2. Draw the bridge.
3. Label consonants on the bridge.
4. Choose pattern and break the word.
5. Repeat for any other syllables.
6. Label the syllable.

cl | cl | op
gravity
VC|VC|V

New Words

gravity

sympathy

Kentucky

Review

patchy

sketchy

pitchy

Break BEFORE you read

grav/it/y
sympathy
Kentucky
patchy
sketchy
pitchy

Break WHILE you read

We felt un/luck/y when gravity made the rocket fall from the sky.

We all felt sympathy for our squad who lost in Kentucky.

Follow the steps to divide the syllables.
1. Label the first two vowels.
2. Draw the bridge.
3. Label consonants on the bridge.
4. Choose pattern and break the word.
5. Repeat for any other syllables.
6. Label the syllable.

Review

New Words

gravity

patchy

sympathy

sketchy

Kentucky

pitchy

Break BEFORE you read

gravity
sympathy
Kentucky
patchy
sketchy
pitchy

Break WHILE you read

We felt unlucky when gravity made the rocket fall from the sky.

We all felt sympathy for our squad who lost in Kentucky.

Activity Set 16

Syllable Type Focus: Magic E

Scope and Sequence

Activity Number	Syllable Pattern	1st Syllable Type	2nd Syllable Type	3rd Syllable Type	Phonics
1	VC/V	Cl	ME	X	Single Phonemes
2	VC/V	Cl	ME	X	Blends & Digraphs
3	VC/V	Cl	ME	X	Blends & Digraphs
4	VC/V	Cl	Cl	ME	Single Phonemes
5	VC/V	Cl	Cl	ME	Blends & Digraphs

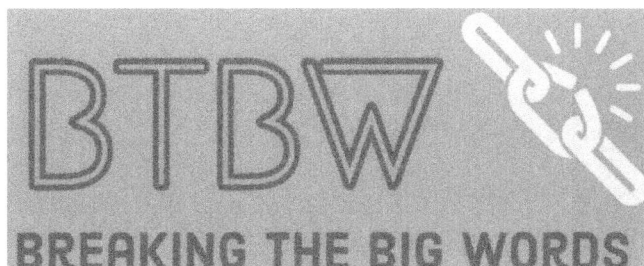

BTBW
BREAKING THE BIG WORDS

Name: _____

Follow the steps to divide the syllables.
1. Label the first two vowels.
2. Draw the bridge.
3. Label consonants on the bridge.
4. Choose pattern and break the word.
5. Repeat for any other syllables.
6. Label the syllable.

cl   me
v o l u m e
V c V

New
Words

☐ ☐
volume
☐

☐ ☐
module
☐

☐ ☐
deluge
☐

☐ ☐
misuse
☐

☐ ☐
exile
☐

☐ ☐
fixate
☐

Break BEFORE you read

vol/ume
misuse
module
exile
deluge
fixate

Break WHILE you read

Why did the she fix/ate so much on the robin's volume?

The misuse of the module led to a deluge of advice.

Follow the steps to divide the syllables.
1. Label the first two vowels.
2. Draw the bridge.
3. Label consonants on the bridge.
4. Choose pattern and break the word.
5. Repeat for any other syllables.
6. Label the syllable.

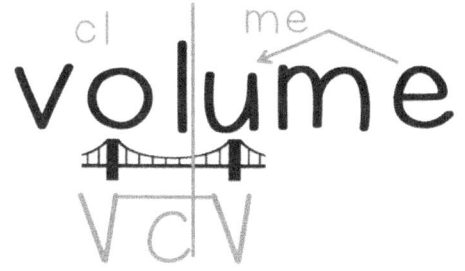

volume

New Words

volume   misuse

module   exile

deluge   fixate

Break BEFORE you read

vol/ume
misuse
module
exile
deluge
fixate

Break WHILE you read

Why did the she fix/ate so much on the robin's volume?

The misuse of the module led to a deluge of advice.

<u>Follow the steps to divide the syllables.</u>
1. Label the first two vowels.
2. Draw the bridge.
3. Label consonants on the bridge.
4. Choose pattern and break the word.
5. Repeat for any other syllables.
6. Label the syllable.

New
Words

volume   misuse

module   exile

deluge   fixate

Break BEFORE you read   Break WHILE you read

volume   Why did the she fixate
misuse   so much on the robin's
module   volume?
exile
deluge   The misuse of the
fixate   module led to a deluge
                         of advice.

Follow the steps to divide the syllables.
1. Label the first two vowels.
2. Draw the bridge.
3. Label consonants on the bridge.
4. Choose pattern and break the word.
5. Repeat for any other syllables.
6. Label the syllable.

grapheme

New
Words

grapheme

schedule

cathode

blockade

Review

satire

exude

Break BEFORE you read

graph/eme
schedule
cathode
blockade
satire
exude

Break WHILE you read

Will we stop the
drag/on with second
blockade?

The cabin schedule on
the ticket was not
what we had hoped.

Follow the steps to divide the syllables.
1. Label the first two vowels.
2. Draw the bridge.
3. Label consonants on the bridge.
4. Choose pattern and break the word.
5. Repeat for any other syllables.
6. Label the syllable.

grapheme

grapheme   schedule

New
Words

cathode   blockade

Review

satire   exude

Break BEFORE you read   Break WHILE you read

graph/eme   Will we stop the
schedule   drag/on with second
cathode   blockade?
blockade
satire   The cabin schedule on
exude   the ticket was not
                        what we had hoped.

<u>Follow the steps to divide the syllables.</u>
1. Label the first two vowels.
2. Draw the bridge.
3. Label consonants on the bridge.
4. Choose pattern and break the word.
5. Repeat for any other syllables.
6. Label the syllable.

New
Words

grapheme   schedule

cathode   blockade

Review

satire   exude

Break BEFORE you read

grapheme
schedule
cathode
blockade
satire
exude

Break WHILE you read

Will we stop the
dragon with second
blockade?

The cabin schedule on
the ticket was not
what we had hoped.

Follow the steps to divide the syllables.
1. Label the first two vowels.
2. Draw the bridge.
3. Label consonants on the bridge.
4. Choose pattern and break the word.
5. Repeat for any other syllables.
6. Label the syllable.

cl   me
tribute
VCV

New Words

tribute

statute

tribune

granite

Review

figure

disuse

Break BEFORE you read

trib/ute
statute
tribune
granite
figure
disuse

Break WHILE you read

The trib/ute to the class camel was a figure made of granite.

The old statute did not allow children to have dragons as pets.

50

Follow the steps to divide the syllables.
1. Label the first two vowels.
2. Draw the bridge.
3. Label consonants on the bridge.
4. Choose pattern and break the word.
5. Repeat for any other syllables.
6. Label the syllable.

cl   me
tribute
VC|V

New
Words

tribute   statute

tribune   granite

Review
figure   disuse

Break BEFORE you read   Break WHILE you read

trib/ute   The trib/ute to the
statute   class camel was a
tribune   figure made of
granite   granite.
figure
disuse   The old statute did not
                             allow children to have
                             dragons as pets.

Follow the steps to divide the syllables.
1. Label the first two vowels.
2. Draw the bridge.
3. Label consonants on the bridge.
4. Choose pattern and break the word.
5. Repeat for any other syllables.
6. Label the syllable.

tribute   statute

New
Words

tribune   granite

Review
figure   disuse

Break BEFORE you read   Break WHILE you read

tribute   The tribute to the class
statute   camel was a figure
tribune   made of granite.
granite
figure   The old statute did not
disuse   allow children to have
                           dragons as pets.

Follow the steps to divide the syllables.
1. Label the first two vowels.
2. Draw the bridge.
3. Label consonants on the bridge.
4. Choose pattern and break the word.
5. Repeat for any other syllables.
6. Label the syllable.

cl | cl | me
customize
V C C V C V

New Words

□ □ □
customize
[   ]

□ □ □
envelope
[   ]

□ □ □
lemonade
[   ]

Review

□ □
legume
[   ]

□ □
graphene
[   ]

□ □
decade
[   ]

Break BEFORE you read

cus/tom/ize
envelope
lemonade
legume
graphene
decade

Break WHILE you read

You can cus/tom/ize the envelope's color and size.

That is the best lemonade I have had in a decade!

Follow the steps to divide the syllables.
1. Label the first two vowels.
2. Draw the bridge.
3. Label consonants on the bridge.
4. Choose pattern and break the word.
5. Repeat for any other syllables.
6. Label the syllable.

cl   cl   me
customize
V C C V C V

New Words

customize

envelope

lemonade

Review

legume

graphene

decade

Break BEFORE you read

cus/tom/ize
envelope
lemonade
legume
graphene
decade

Break WHILE you read

You can cus/tom/ize the envelope's color and size.

That is the best lemonade I have had in a decade!

Follow the steps to divide the syllables.

1. Label the first two vowels.
2. Draw the bridge.
3. Label consonants on the bridge.
4. Choose pattern and break the word.
5. Repeat for any other syllables.
6. Label the syllable.

New Words

Review

customize

legume

envelope

graphene

lemonade

decade

Break BEFORE you read

customize
envelope
lemonade
legume
graphene
decade

Break WHILE you read

You can customize the envelope's color and size.

That is the best lemonade I have had in a decade!

Follow the steps to divide the syllables.
1. Label the first two vowels.
2. Draw the bridge.
3. Label consonants on the bridge.
4. Choose pattern and break the word.
5. Repeat for any other syllables.
6. Label the syllable.

cl | cl | me
dis**t**ribute
V|C|C|V|C|V

New Words

di**s**tribute

randomize

magnetize

Review

stockade

stylize

globule

Break BEFORE you read

dis/trib/ute
randomize
magnetize
stockade
stylize
globule

Break WHILE you read

I had to mag/net/ize this pen in my pocket for the magic trick.

If we distribute the work, we will finish with time to spare.

Name: _____

Follow the steps to divide the syllables.
1. Label the first two vowels.
2. Draw the bridge.
3. Label consonants on the bridge.
4. Choose pattern and break the word.
5. Repeat for any other syllables.
6. Label the syllable.

cl   cl   me
di**s**t**r**ib**u**te
VC C VC V

New Words

dis<u>tr</u>ibute

randomize

magnetize

Review

<u>st</u>ockade

<u>st</u>ylize

<u>gl</u>obule

Break BEFORE you read

dis/trib/ute
randomize
magnetize
stockade
stylize
globule

Break WHILE you read

I had to mag/net/ize this pen in my pocket for the magic trick.

If we distribute the work, we will finish with time to spare.

Follow the steps to divide the syllables.
1. Label the first two vowels.
2. Draw the bridge.
3. Label consonants on the bridge.
4. Choose pattern and break the word.
5. Repeat for any other syllables.
6. Label the syllable.

New Words

Review

distribute   stockade

randomize   stylize

magnetize   globule

Break BEFORE you read

distribute
randomize
magnetize
stockade
stylize
globule

Break WHILE you read

I had to magnetize this pen in my pocket for the magic trick.

If we distribute the work, we will finish with time to spare.

Activity Set 17

Syllable Type Focus: Vowel Pairs

Scope and Sequence

Activity Number	Syllable Pattern	1st Syllable Type	2nd Syllable Type	3rd Syllable Type	Phonics
1	VC/V	Cl & VP	Op & ME	X	Single Phonemes
2	VC/V	VP	Cl, Op & VP	X	Blends & Digraphs
3	VC/V	VP	Cl & Op	X	Blends & Digraphs
4	VC/V	Cl	Cl & VP	Cl & VP	Single Phonemes
5	VC/V	Cl	VP	Cl	Blends & Digraphs

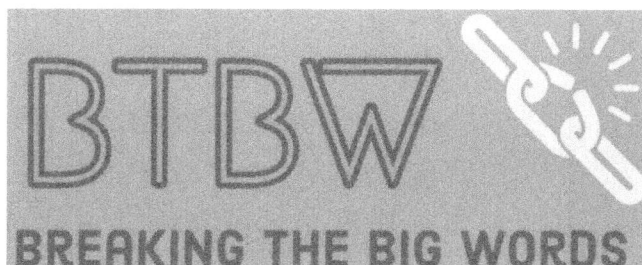

BTBW
BREAKING THE BIG WORDS

Follow the steps to divide the syllables.
1. Label the first two vowels.
2. Draw the bridge.
3. Label consonants on the bridge.
4. Choose pattern and break the word.
5. Repeat for any other syllables.
6. Label the syllable.

c l   V P

value

V C V

New
Words

☐ ☐

v a l u̲e̲

☐

☐ ☐

w e̲a̲ry

☐

☐ ☐

d a̲i̲ry

☐

☐ ☐

v e n u̲e̲

☐

☐ ☐

e̲a̲sy

☐

☐ ☐

l e̲e̲ry

☐

Break BEFORE you read

val/ue
venue
weary
easy
dairy
leery

Break WHILE you read

The val/ue of the venue
was much more than we
thought it would be.

We were leery of the
dairy after it was in the
sun for so long.

Follow the steps to divide the syllables.
1. Label the first two vowels.
2. Draw the bridge.
3. Label consonants on the bridge.
4. Choose pattern and break the word.
5. Repeat for any other syllables.
6. Label the syllable.

value

New
Words

value   venue

weary   easy

dairy   leery

Break BEFORE you read   Break WHILE you read

val/ue   The val/ue of the venue
venue   was much more than we
weary   thought it would be.
easy
dairy   We were leery of the
leery   dairy after it was in the
                         sun for so long.

Follow the steps to divide the syllables.
1. Label the first two vowels.
2. Draw the bridge.
3. Label consonants on the bridge.
4. Choose pattern and break the word.
5. Repeat for any other syllables.
6. Label the syllable.

New
Words

value   venue

weary   easy

dairy   leery

Break BEFORE you read   Break WHILE you read

value   The value of the venue
venue   was much more than we
weary   thought it would be.
easy
dairy   We were leery of the
leery   dairy after it was in the
                         sun for so long.

Name: _____

Follow the steps to divide the syllables.
1. Label the first two vowels.
2. Draw the bridge.
3. Label consonants on the bridge.
4. Choose pattern and break the word.
5. Repeat for any other syllables.
6. Label the syllable.

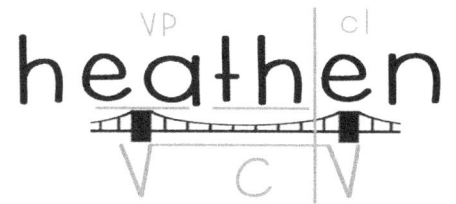

heathen

New Words

heathen

greedy

Review

goalie

sheepish

sneaky

needy

Break BEFORE you read

heath/en
sheepish
greedy
sneaky
goalie
needy

Break WHILE you read

The jock/ey was sheepish with the sneaky horse.

The goalie dove and made it to the hockey puck just in time.

Name: _____

Follow the steps to divide the syllables.
1. Label the first two vowels.
2. Draw the bridge.
3. Label consonants on the bridge.
4. Choose pattern and break the word.
5. Repeat for any other syllables.
6. Label the syllable.

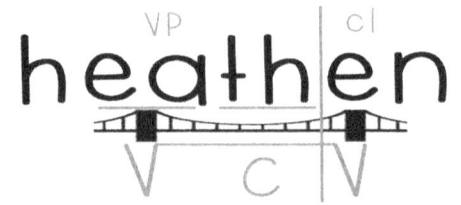

heathen

New
Words

heathen   sheepish

greedy   sneaky

Review

goalie   needy

Break BEFORE you read

heath/en
sheepish
greedy
sneaky
goalie
needy

Break WHILE you read

The jock/ey was
sheepish with the
sneaky horse.

The goalie dove and
made it to the hockey
puck just in time.

Follow the steps to divide the syllables.
1. Label the first two vowels.
2. Draw the bridge.
3. Label consonants on the bridge.
4. Choose pattern and break the word.
5. Repeat for any other syllables.
6. Label the syllable.

New
Words

heathen   sheepish

greedy   sneaky

Review

goalie   needy

Break BEFORE you read   Break WHILE you read

heathen   The jockey was
sheepish   sheepish with the
greedy   sneaky horse.
sneaky
goalie   The goalie dove and
needy   made it to the hockey
                               puck just in time.

Name: _____

Follow the steps to divide the syllables.
1. Label the first two vowels.
2. Draw the bridge.
3. Label consonants on the bridge.
4. Choose pattern and break the word.
5. Repeat for any other syllables.
6. Label the syllable.

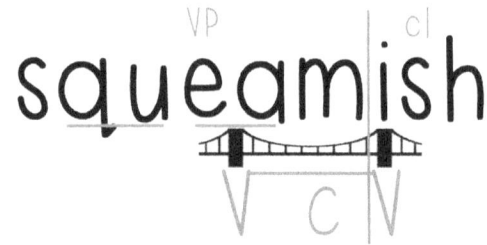

VP | cl
s q u e a m i s h
V | C | V

New
Words

☐ ☐
<u>squ</u>eamish
☐☐☐☐

☐ ☐
<u>sp</u>eedy
☐☐☐☐

☐ ☐
<u>gr</u>eenish
☐☐☐☐

☐ ☐
<u>pr</u>eaching
☐☐☐☐

Review

☐ ☐
<u>a</u>i<u>r</u>y
☐☐☐☐

☐ ☐
<u>t</u>oady
☐☐☐☐

Break BEFORE you read

squeam/ish
speedy
greenish
preaching
airy
toady

Break WHILE you read

The speed/y robin shot through the city to get to his tree.

Did you see the squeamish camel turn a greenish shade?

Follow the steps to divide the syllables.
1. Label the first two vowels.
2. Draw the bridge.
3. Label consonants on the bridge.
4. Choose pattern and break the word.
5. Repeat for any other syllables.
6. Label the syllable.

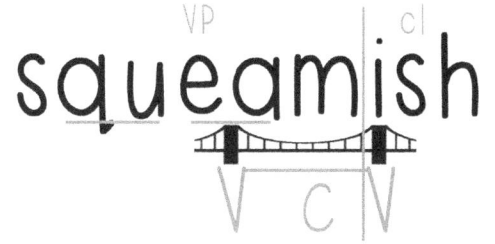

squeamish

squeamish   speedy

New
Words

greenish   preaching

Review

airy   toady

Break BEFORE you read

squeam/ish
speedy
greenish
preaching
airy
toady

Break WHILE you read

The speed/y robin shot through the city to get to his tree.

Did you see the squeamish camel turn a greenish shade?

Follow the steps to divide the syllables.
1. Label the first two vowels.
2. Draw the bridge.
3. Label consonants on the bridge.
4. Choose pattern and break the word.
5. Repeat for any other syllables.
6. Label the syllable.

squeamish   **speedy**

New
Words

greenish   **preaching**

Review

airy   **today**

Break BEFORE you read

squeamish
speedy
greenish
preaching
airy
toady

Break WHILE you read

The speedy robin shot through the city to get to his tree.

Did you see the squeamish camel turn a greenish shade?

Follow the steps to divide the syllables.
1. Label the first two vowels.
2. Draw the bridge.
3. Label consonants on the bridge.
4. Choose pattern and break the word.
5. Repeat for any other syllables.
6. Label the syllable.

con|tin|ue
VC CVC V

New Words

☐ ☐ ☐

continue

☐ ☐ ☐

velveteen

☐ ☐ ☐

upheaval

Review

☐ ☐

levee

☐ ☐

seedy

☐ ☐

meaty

Break BEFORE you read

con/tin/ue
velveteen
upheaval
levee
seedy
meaty

Break WHILE you read

Can we con/tin/ue to read The Velveteen Rabbit?

Upheaval in the creek's water level was too much for the levee.

Follow the steps to divide the syllables.
1. Label the first two vowels.
2. Draw the bridge.
3. Label consonants on the bridge.
4. Choose pattern and break the word.
5. Repeat for any other syllables.
6. Label the syllable.

cl cl VP
con|tin|ue
V C|C V C|V

New Words

Review

continue

levee

velveteen

seedy

upheaval

meaty

Break BEFORE you read

con/tin/ue
velveteen
upheaval
levee
seedy
meaty

Break WHILE you read

Can we con/tin/ue to read The Velveteen Rabbit?

Upheaval in the creek's water level was too much for the levee.

Follow the steps to divide the syllables.
1. Label the first two vowels.
2. Draw the bridge.
3. Label consonants on the bridge.
4. Choose pattern and break the word.
5. Repeat for any other syllables.
6. Label the syllable.

New Words

Review

continue

levee

velveteen

seedy

upheaval

meaty

Break BEFORE you read

continue
velveteen
upheaval
levee
seedy
meaty

Break WHILE you read

Can we continue to read The Velveteen Rabbit?

Upheaval in the creek's water level was too much for the levee.

Follow the steps to divide the syllables.
1. Label the first two vowels.
2. Draw the bridge.
3. Label consonants on the bridge.
4. Choose pattern and break the word.
5. Repeat for any other syllables.
6. Label the syllable.

cl   VP   cl
exclaiming
V C C V C V

Review

New Words

☐ ☐ ☐
exclaiming
[ ]

☐ ☐ ☐
appraisal
[ ]

☐ ☐
unfeeling
[ ]

☐ ☐
peevish
[ ]

☐ ☐
teary
[ ]

☐ ☐
dreary
[ ]

Break BEFORE you read
ex/claim/ing
appraisal
unfeeling
peevish
teary
dreary

Break WHILE you read
The goalie was ex/claim/ing that no ball will get past him.

We found the second team unfeeling but athletic.

Follow the steps to divide the syllables.
1. Label the first two vowels.
2. Draw the bridge.
3. Label consonants on the bridge.
4. Choose pattern and break the word.
5. Repeat for any other syllables.
6. Label the syllable.

cl | VP | cl
exclaiming
VC|C V C|V

New Words

exclaiming

appraisal

unfeeling

Review

peevish

teary

dreary

Break BEFORE you read
ex/claim/ing
appraisal
unfeeling
peevish
teary
dreary

Break WHILE you read
The goalie was ex/claim/ing that no ball will get past him.

We found the second team unfeeling but athletic.

Follow the steps to divide the syllables.
1. Label the first two vowels.
2. Draw the bridge.
3. Label consonants on the bridge.
4. Choose pattern and break the word.
5. Repeat for any other syllables.
6. Label the syllable.

New Words

exclaiming

appraisal

unfeeling

Review

peevish

teary

dreary

Break BEFORE you read

exclaiming
appraisal
unfeeling
peevish
teary
dreary

Break WHILE you read

The goalie was exclaiming that no ball will get past him.

We found the second team unfeeling but athletic.

Activity Set 18

Syllable Type Focus: Bossy R /er/

Scope and Sequence

Activity Number	Syllable Pattern	1st Syllable Type	2nd Syllable Type	3rd Syllable Type	Phonics
1	VC/V	Cl, BR, & VP	Cl & BR	X	Single Phonemes
2	VC/V	Cl & VP	BR	X	Blends & Digraphs
3	VC/V	Cl, BR, & VP	Cl & BR	X	Blends & Digraphs
4	VC/V	Cl	Cl & BR	Cl & BR	Single Phonemes
5	VC/V	Cl	Cl	BR	Blends & Digraphs

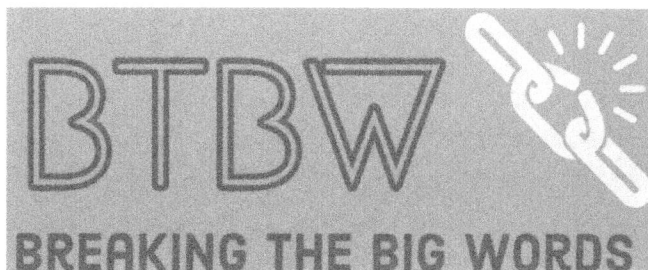

BTBW
BREAKING THE BIG WORDS

Follow the steps to divide the syllables.
1. Label the first two vowels.
2. Draw the bridge.
3. Label consonants on the bridge.
4. Choose pattern and break the word.
5. Repeat for any other syllables.
6. Label the syllable.

cl   BR
r i v|e r
V c|V

☐ ☐

river

☐

New
Words

☐ ☐

beeper

☐

☐ ☐

deeper

☐

☐ ☐

loafer

☐

☐ ☐

keeper

☐

☐ ☐

forum

☐

Break BEFORE you read

riv/er
loafer
beeper
keeper
deeper
forum

Break WHILE you read

We were luck/y we did not go into the deeper part of the river.

The sheepish keeper could not get to the ball in time.

76

Follow the steps to divide the syllables.
1. Label the first two vowels.
2. Draw the bridge.
3. Label consonants on the bridge.
4. Choose pattern and break the word.
5. Repeat for any other syllables.
6. Label the syllable.

cl   BR
ri v/e r
V c V

river   loafer

New
Words

beeper   keeper

deeper   forum

Break BEFORE you read   Break WHILE you read

riv/er   We were luck/y we did
loafer   not go into the deeper
beeper   part of the river.
keeper
deeper   The sheepish keeper
forum   could not get to the
                ball in time.

<u>Follow the steps to divide the syllables.</u>
1. Label the first two vowels.
2. Draw the bridge.
3. Label consonants on the bridge.
4. Choose pattern and break the word.
5. Repeat for any other syllables.
6. Label the syllable.

New
Words

river   loafer

beeper   keeper

deeper   forum

Break BEFORE you read

river
loafer
beeper
keeper
deeper
forum

Break WHILE you read

We were lucky we did not go into the deeper part of the river.

The sheepish keeper could not get to the ball in time.

Follow the steps to divide the syllables.

1. Label the first two vowels.
2. Draw the bridge.
3. Label consonants on the bridge.
4. Choose pattern and break the word.
5. Repeat for any other syllables.
6. Label the syllable.

cl   BR

us|her

V   C   V

New
Words

usher

shiver

Review

ever

tether

squeaker

waiver

Break BEFORE you read

ush/er
tether
shiver
squeaker
ever
waiver

Break WHILE you read

The ush/er took us to our seats at the venue.

That game of tether ball was a real squeaker!

Name: _____

Follow the steps to divide the syllables.
1. Label the first two vowels.
2. Draw the bridge.
3. Label consonants on the bridge.
4. Choose pattern and break the word.
5. Repeat for any other syllables.
6. Label the syllable.

cl   BR
u s h | e r
V   C | V

New
Words

usher   tether

shiver   squeaker

Review

ever   waiver

Break BEFORE you read   Break WHILE you read

ush/er   The ush/er took us to
tether   our seats at the venue.
shiver
squeaker   That game of tether
ever   ball was a real
waiver   squeaker!

<u>Follow the steps to divide the syllables.</u>
1. Label the first two vowels.
2. Draw the bridge.
3. Label consonants on the bridge.
4. Choose pattern and break the word.
5. Repeat for any other syllables.
6. Label the syllable.

New
Words

usher   tether

shiver   squeaker

Review

ever   waiver

Break BEFORE you read   Break WHILE you read

usher   The usher took us to
tether   our seats at the venue.
shiver
squeaker   That game of tether
ever   ball was a real
waiver   squeaker!

Follow the steps to divide the syllables.
1. Label the first two vowels.
2. Draw the bridge.
3. Label consonants on the bridge.
4. Choose pattern and break the word.
5. Repeat for any other syllables.
6. Label the syllable.

BR   cl
forest
V c V

□ □
forest
▭

□ □
cavern
▭

New
Words

□ □
sliver
▭

□ □
speaker
▭

Review

□ □
whether
▭

□ □
never
▭

Break BEFORE you read

for/est
cavern
sliver
speaker
whether
never

Break WHILE you read

We went deep/er into the forest and found a huge cave.

Have you ever been that deep in a cavern?

Follow the steps to divide the syllables.
1. Label the first two vowels.
2. Draw the bridge.
3. Label consonants on the bridge.
4. Choose pattern and break the word.
5. Repeat for any other syllables.
6. Label the syllable.

BR   cl

for|est

V C V

New Words

fore<u>st</u>   cave<u>rn</u>

<u>sl</u>iver   <u>sp</u>eaker

Review

<u>wh</u>e<u>th</u>er   never

Break BEFORE you read

for/est
cavern
sliver
speaker
whether
never

Break WHILE you read

We went deep/er into the forest and found a huge cave.

Have you ever been that deep in a cavern?

Follow the steps to divide the syllables.
1. Label the first two vowels.
2. Draw the bridge.
3. Label consonants on the bridge.
4. Choose pattern and break the word.
5. Repeat for any other syllables.
6. Label the syllable.

New
Words

forest   cavern

sliver   speaker

Review

whether   never

Break BEFORE you read

forest
cavern
sliver
speaker
whether
never

Break WHILE you read

We went deeper into the forest and found a huge cave.

Have you ever been that deep in a cavern?

Follow the steps to divide the syllables.
1. Label the first two vowels.
2. Draw the bridge.
3. Label consonants on the bridge.
4. Choose pattern and break the word.
5. Repeat for any other syllables.
6. Label the syllable.

cl   BR   cl
his t or ic
V C C V C V

New Words

☐ ☐ ☐
historic
☐

☐ ☐ ☐
general
☐

☐ ☐ ☐
deliver
☐

Review

☐ ☐
sweeper
☐

☐ ☐
clever
☐

☐ ☐
quiver
☐

Break BEFORE you read

his/tor/ic
general
deliver
sweeper
clever
quiver

Break WHILE you read

The battle led by this gen/er/al was historic.

If we are clever, we can deliver the gifts in one day.

Follow the steps to divide the syllables.
1. Label the first two vowels.
2. Draw the bridge.
3. Label consonants on the bridge.
4. Choose pattern and break the word.
5. Repeat for any other syllables.
6. Label the syllable.

cl   BR   cl
his tor ic
V C | C V C | V

New Words

Review

historic

sweeper

general

clever

deliver

quiver

Break BEFORE you read

his/tor/ic
general
deliver
sweeper
clever
quiver

Break WHILE you read

The battle led by this gen/er/al was historic.

If we are clever, we can deliver the gifts in one day.

<u>Follow the steps to divide the syllables.</u>
1. Label the first two vowels.
2. Draw the bridge.
3. Label consonants on the bridge.
4. Choose pattern and break the word.
5. Repeat for any other syllables.
6. Label the syllable.

New Words

Review

historic

sweeper

general

clever

deliver

quiver

Break BEFORE you read
historic
general
deliver
sweeper
clever
quiver

Break WHILE you read

The battle led by this general was historic.

If we are clever, we can deliver the gifts in one day.

Name: _____

Follow the steps to divide the syllables.
1. Label the first two vowels.
2. Draw the bridge.
3. Label consonants on the bridge.
4. Choose pattern and break the word.
5. Repeat for any other syllables.
6. Label the syllable.

wh**e**n**e**v**e**r
V C V C V

New Words

whenever

whichever

another

Review

sneaker

sleeper

creeper

Break BEFORE you read

when/ev/er
whichever
another
sneaker
sleeper
creeper

Break WHILE you read

Which/ev/er pair of sneakers you pick will work just fine.

Whenever we find another speaker we can set up the present.

88

Follow the steps to divide the syllables.
1. Label the first two vowels.
2. Draw the bridge.
3. Label consonants on the bridge.
4. Choose pattern and break the word.
5. Repeat for any other syllables.
6. Label the syllable.

cl   cl   BR
whenever
V C V C V

New Words   ## Review

<u>wh</u>enever   <u>sn</u>eaker

<u>wh</u>ichever   <u>sl</u>eeper

ano<u>th</u>er   <u>cr</u>eeper

Break BEFORE you read   ### Break WHILE you read

when/ev/er   Which/ev/er pair of
whichever   sneakers you pick will
another   work just fine.
sneaker
sleeper   Whenever we find
creeper   another speaker we
                         can set up the present.

Follow the steps to divide the syllables.
1. Label the first two vowels.
2. Draw the bridge.
3. Label consonants on the bridge.
4. Choose pattern and break the word.
5. Repeat for any other syllables.
6. Label the syllable.

New Words

Review

whenever

sneaker

whichever

sleeper

another

creeper

Break BEFORE you read

whenever
whichever
another
sneaker
sleeper
creeper

Break WHILE you read

Whichever pair of sneakers you pick will work just fine.

Whenever we find another speaker we can set up the present.

Activity Set
14

Syllabication Anchor Word Posters

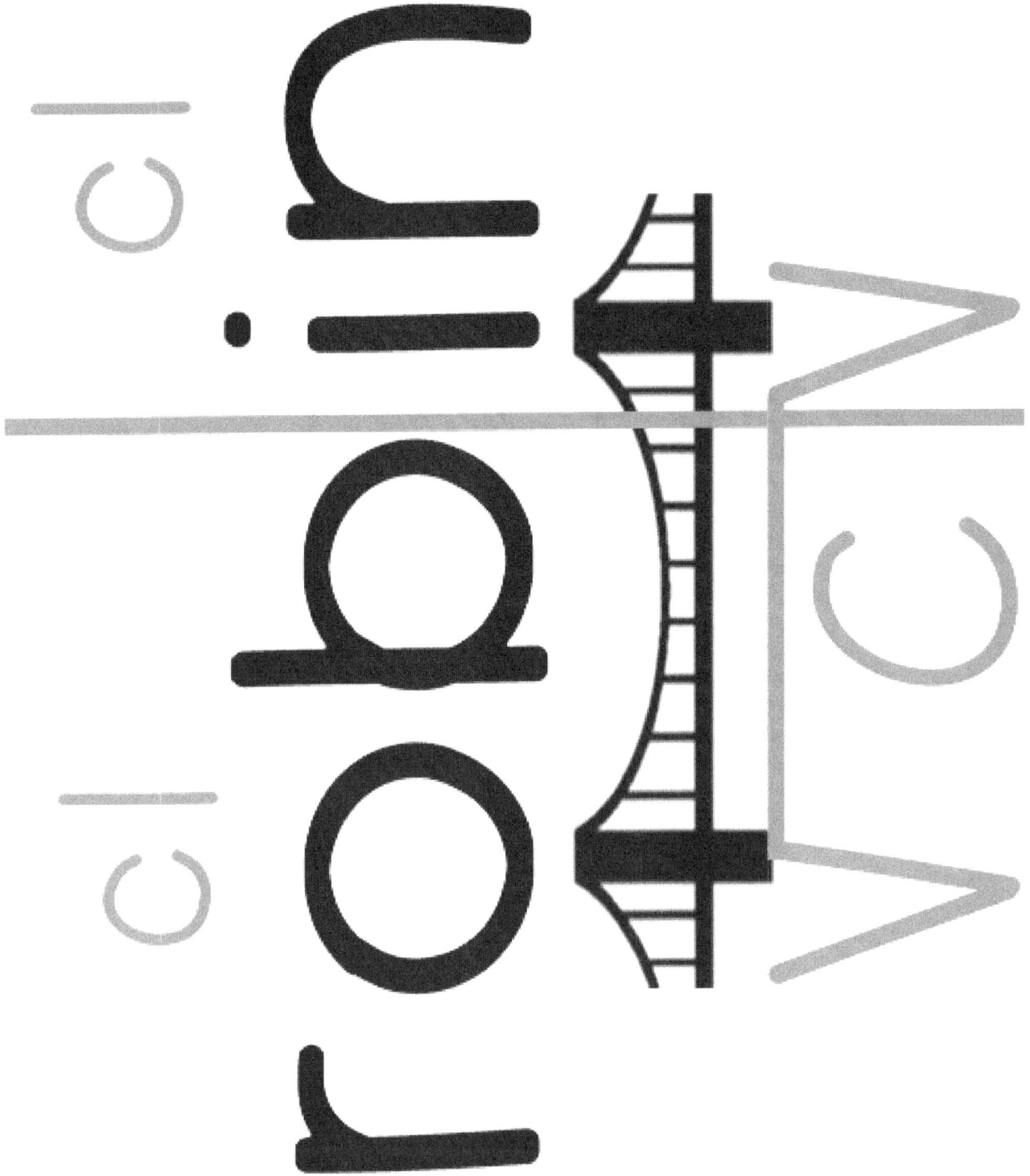

dragon

pocket NC

volcanic

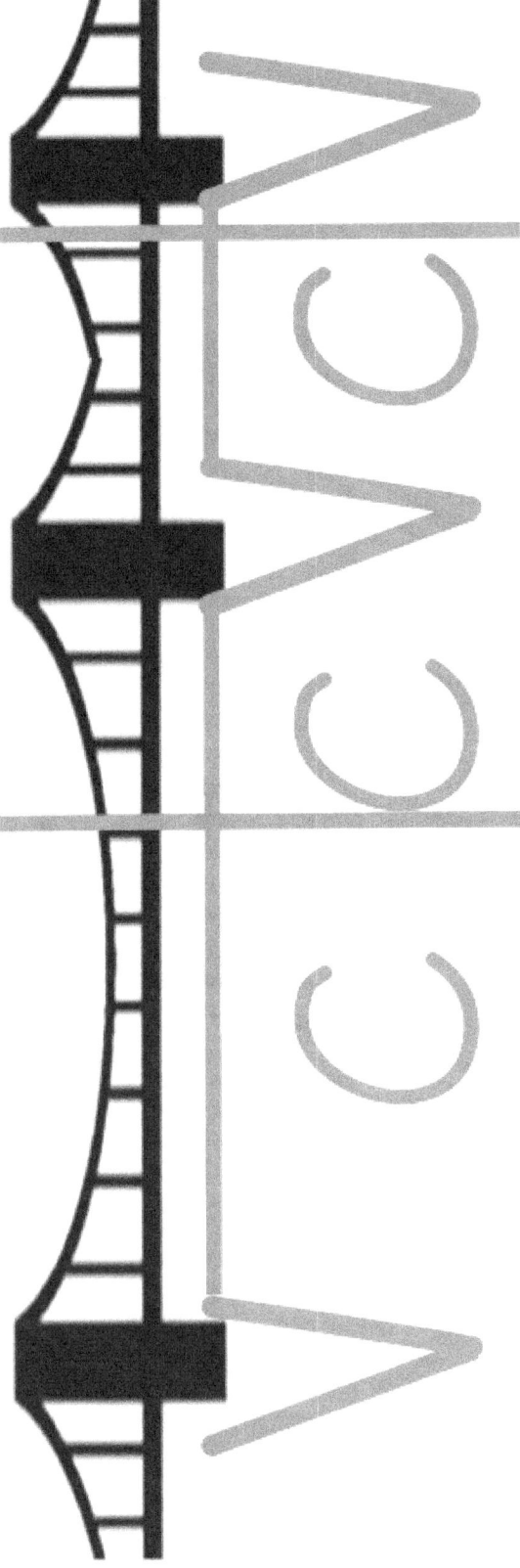

athletic

Syllabication Anchor Word Posters

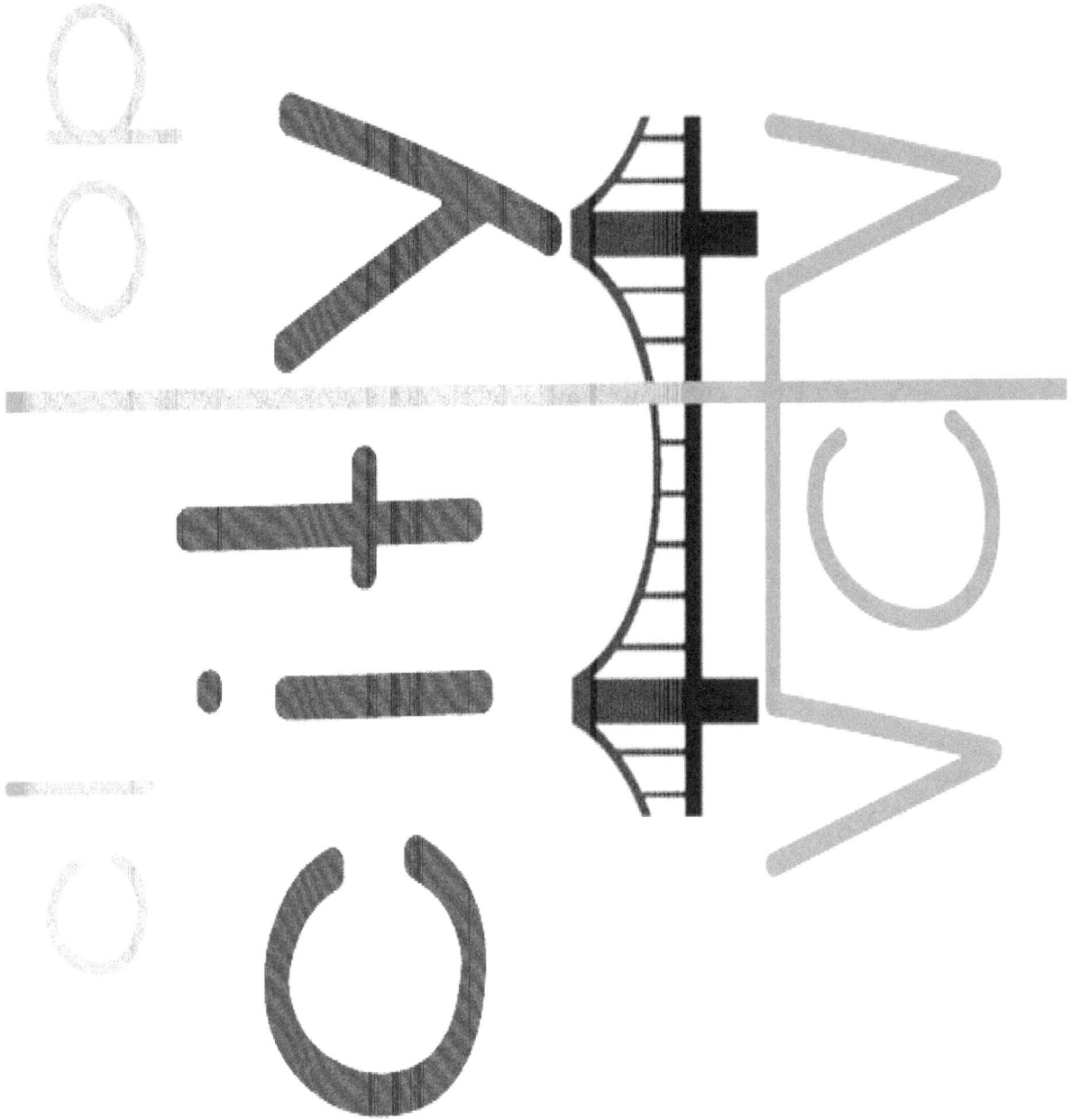

cl | op

study

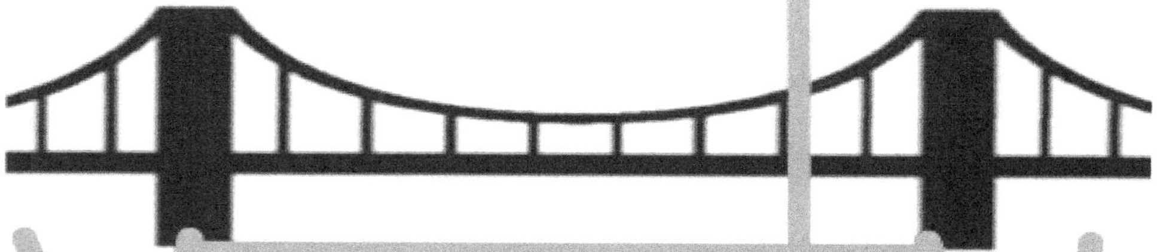

V C | V

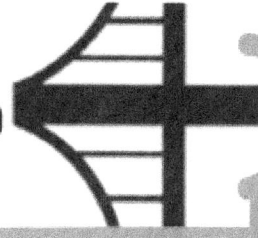

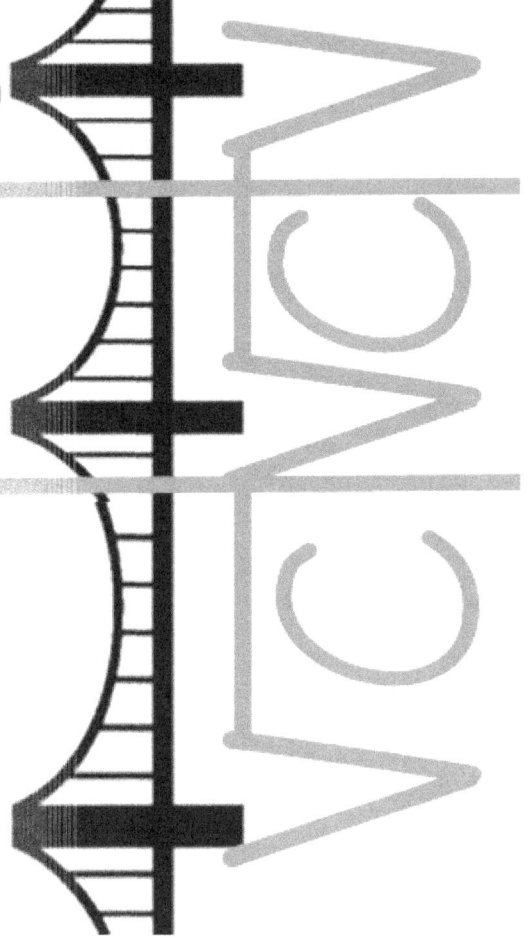

gravity

loop

elastic loop

Activity Set
16

Syllabication Anchor Word Posters

volume

me

cl

grapheme

cl

me

√ C C

customize

me

cl cl cl

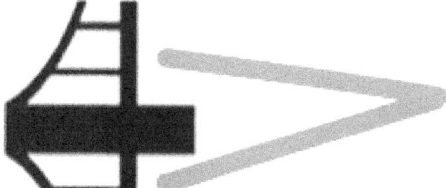

VCVCVC

me

cl cl

cl cl

distribute

VCCVCVC

Activity Set
17

Syllabication Anchor Word Posters

value

VP

VC

heathen

squeamish

continue

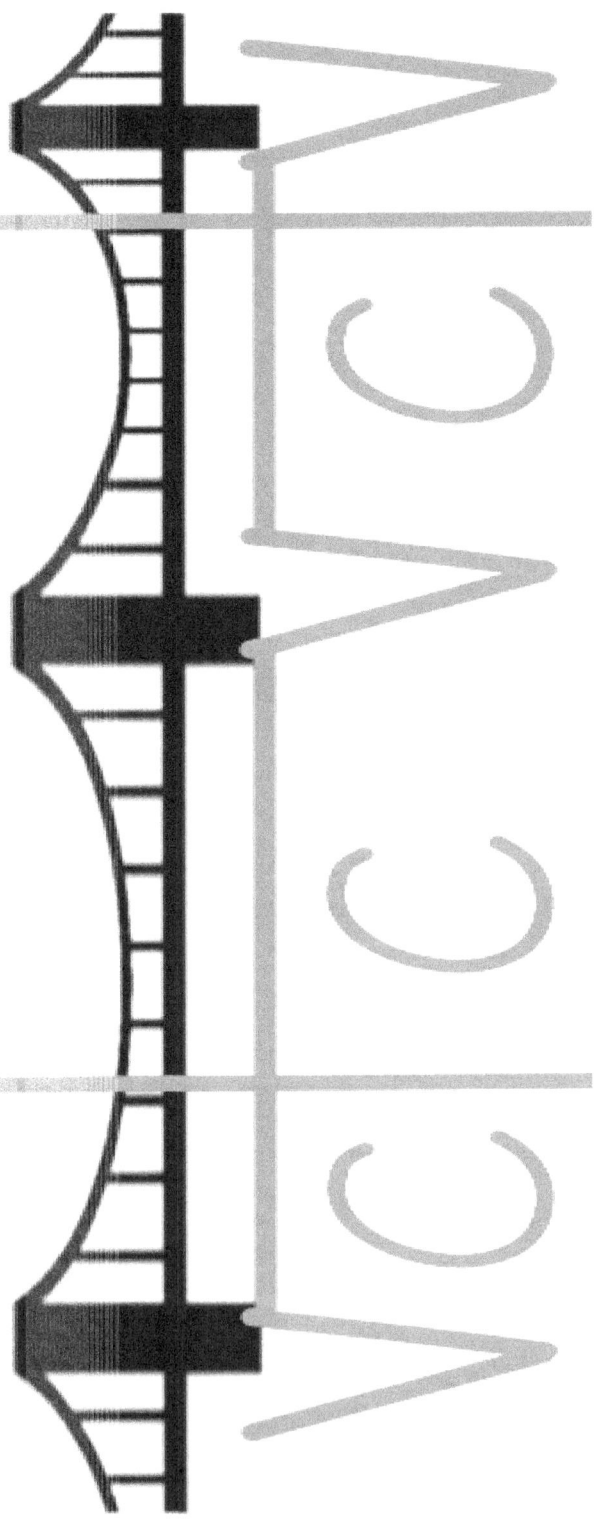

exclaiming

VC CVC CVCN

Activity Set 18

Syllabication Anchor Word Posters

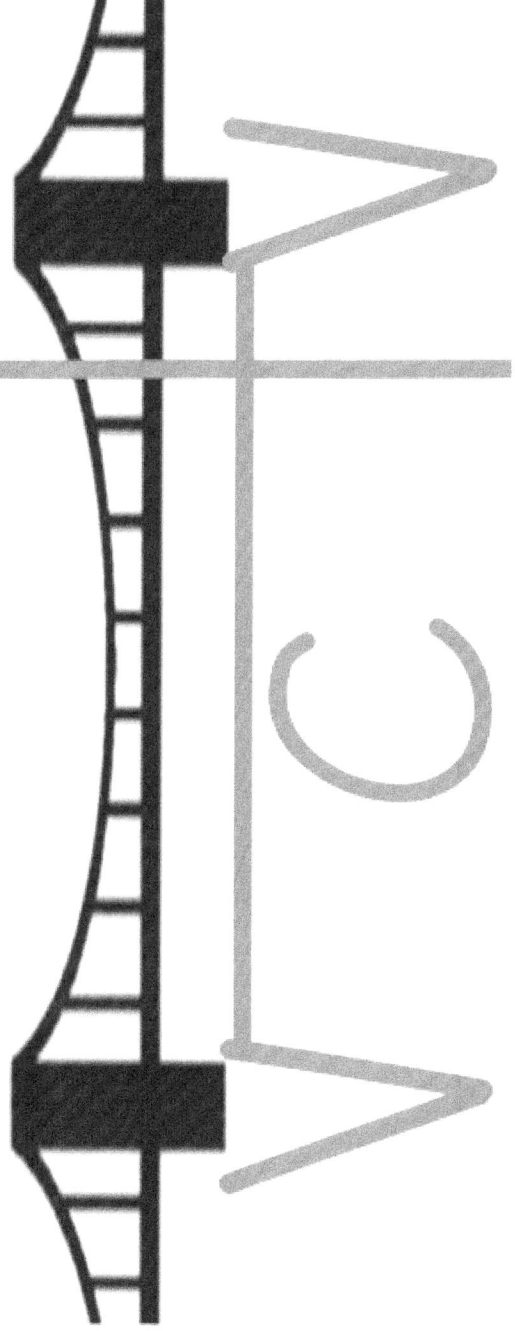

test

forest

BRIDGE

CITY

historic
BR
VICTORIC

cl cl BR

cl cl cl

whenever

VCVCV

VC VCV

Vowel Types

Long	Short	Tricksters
Name of vowel	Sound of vowel	Different
wait line so	hat up top	town coin lawn

Dividing Syllables

1 Label 2 vowels
2 Draw bridge
3 Label C on the bridge
4 Choose Syllable Pattern
5 Split
6 Syllable Type & Label
7 Read or Repeat

LET'S BREAK WORDS!

Syllable Type

Say this to remember!

Rabbits	R	Bossy R
Eat	E	Magic E
Very	V	Vowel Pair
Large	L	Consonant-le
Orange	O	Open
Carrots	C	Closed

Letter Types

VOWELS	CONSONANTS
a e i o u (y)	Every other letter

Syllable Patterns

1. vc/cv	2. v/cv	3. vc/v	4. v/v	5. -cle
1st syllable closed	1st syllable open	1st syllable closed	1st syllable open	
Jum/bo Mag/net Ship/shape	Ra/ven Ro/ver So/lo	Cab/in Rob/ert Gav/in	Ne/on Cre/ate Me/an/der	1st closed: Bot/tle 1st open: No/ble

Thank You

Thank you to From the Pond for the Pond Fonts.
Visit the store on Teachers Pay Teachers.

Thank you to Tracee Orman for the Clip Art Frames.
Visit the store on Teachers Pay Teachers.

Thank you to Creative Clips by Krista Wallden for the
great free font!
Visit her store on Teachers Pay Teachers.

Made in the USA
Las Vegas, NV
09 May 2025

21919300R00070